# DESERT FLO...

*A journey into the feminine
in women, men, and God*

❖❖❖❖❖❖❖❖❖❖❖❖❖❖❖❖❖❖❖❖❖❖❖❖❖❖❖❖❖

## MARY ROBINS

*SHEFFIELD*
CAIRNS PUBLICATIONS
1990

First published 1990

Further copies of this book are obtainable from
Cairns Publications
47 Firth Park Avenue, Sheffield s5 6HF

*Printed by J. W. Northend Ltd*
*Clyde Road, Sheffield s8 OTZ*

Cairns Publications
Dwylan, Stryd Fawr, Harlech,
Gwynedd, LL46 2YA
www.cottercairns.co.uk
office@cottercairns.co.uk

# *CONTENTS*

*For*

Louisa Katharine 1878-1961
Katharine Winifred 1908-
Ann Katherine 1967-

*From*

Mary Katherine 1934-

# PREFACE

If you make my word your home
you will indeed be my disciples,
and you will learn the truth
and the truth will set you free.

*John* 8.32

BELIEVING in Jesus Christ, I set off on a spiritual journey into my own inner wilderness – a blocked, arid desert. The process of my journeying begins through stones of resistance that obstruct the Way, through the blistering heat of anger and the cold of icy fear, through the pain of foot-slogging and of wounds revealed. However, early in my journey green growing things appeared. At first they had both prickles and buds. Then, after flash floods of feelings there were flowers, now and again. Eventually, blossoms were given.

This journey is one of confession, absolution, and the discovery of self-esteem. It leads to a place of creativity, openness, discovery, and hope. The means of 'travel' have been Jungian, Ignatian, intuitive massage, and Tai-Chi. I have been accompanied in turn by spiritual guides, by a masseuse, by family and friends, whose patience, affirmation, and challenge kept me moving.

I wrote first in passionate reflections from my experience and insights. Later, I put the reflections together to make a map of the journey. I claim no literary skills, but I write to share experience of human beings and God. Friends who have read the reflections have encouraged me to share them more widely. As one of them said, "These are everyday experiences of the things we read about in books."

My experience clarifies the understanding that after hundreds, thousands of years of living in a patriarchal system, our Western Civilization has distorted the balance of masculine and feminine in Society and in the Church. We have developed and affirmed roles for women based on men's fears and on men's idealization of women. As a result, we have hidden much real feminine energy in women themselves as well as in men. We have often denied the feminine in men (anima) so that it is weak, self-pitying, or romantic. We have applauded the masculine in women (animus) and then disapproved of the monsters that emerged. It has been assumed that men's experience includes the experience of women. Biologically at least that cannot be so! We have a church tradition of using male imagery for our Infinite God. As we recognize what has happened, we are freer in Christ to be creative with the gifts of masculine and feminine energy in men and women – and between them.

There are more details of the sociology, psychology, and theology of this theme in these books which I recommend.

Brian Wren, *What language shall I borrow?* SCM, 1989
Jim Cotter, *Pleasure, pain and passion.* Cairns, 1988
Paul Avis, *Eros and the sacred.* Crossroads
Genia Pauli Haddon, *Body metaphors.* Crossroads
Sylvia Brinton Perara, *Descent to the goddess – a way of initiation for women.* Inner City.

My deep thanks go to Jill Butt, who listened, encouraged, typed, and helped the book to birth, and to Sheena Barnes for her Foreword. Also my loving appreciation of Brian Robins, who gave me space to grow and write, and of Mark Robins and Richard Robins, who affirmed my growing. My grateful thanks to Jan Russell for her understanding and for her sensitive drawings. Much appreciation of Jenny Padstow's careful editing that didn't hurt at all. My gratitude to Sue Fisk and Rosalie Beach who read and advised, and to John Morris who gave his deacon freedom to explore. Especially, my deep appreciation of Jim Cotter, who listened, affirmed, and published *Desert Flowers*.

The reader's experience will be different from mine, but there will be similar paths, landmarks, and flowers along the way. I willingly share my experience with you and hope some of you will share yours with me, as together we are freed into Truth.

MARY ROBINS
*North Mymms, November* 1989

# FOREWORD

I HAVE enjoyed reading this book of poems, prayers, and meditations. Mary describes an intensely personal journey, through pain, betrayal, fear, battle, therapy, healing, and rebirth. Although personal, the tensions clearly expressed are those of any woman who works within a Church modelled primarily by men. She works through the cloying attitudes of the past, the conflicts around male and female, masculine and feminine, as well as her own inner dilemmas.

We certainly have different perspectives within feminism. But what I admire so much is that she is unafraid to face and work through conflict in her writing. This must be a way forward for us today, whether from within or on the margins of the Church.

SHEENA BARNES
*February* 1990

*Sheena Barnes worked as a Deacon in the Anglican Church from 1986 to 1990. She now paints full-time, and helps others explore the Spirit through art workshops.*

# PRICKLES AND BUDS

# 1 *The gift of tears*

As I moved into the desert, I was often in prickly mood. My guide asked, "What do you feel?" I could not say – I knew only what I ought to feel. With sobs that would not turn to tears, I began the journey to find my own feelings. Gradually, I began to discover them – repressed, denied, hidden deep. And they were released through tears. As I received and shared the gift of tears with men and women, this reflection emerged.

Tears are a gift.
In past ages they were put in a bottle,
and looked at – a memorial . . .
Nowadays,
what do we do with our tears?

We recall a woman who massaged Jesus's feet.
Her professional skill was to give
men's bodies a sensation of being loved.
As she worked,
she felt his tenderness.
As he sat being tested,
probed,
investigated by experts,
she felt him vulnerable.
And she wept –
tears, tears, tears –
and knew forgiveness in herself,
acceptance,
love.

For us too
tears well up from the hollow within,
seep through the skin,
squeezed from our depths,
ozzing sadness,
grieving for what might have been.

Tears make us tender
softening the hard container.

But stop!
An inner voice says,
"Hold them back,
pack them down,
bottle them up."
The inner voice was trained to cope.

A man said,
"You upset me when you cry –
stop it."
Fearing to cause trouble,
to lose his attention,
the aproval that was a substitute for love,
the passive soul trained the body to hide the tears,
saying, "Survive, survive – cope – escape."
A twisted web of love and hate
wove from her to him –
in

        out

            back

round

       tighter

          tighter.

Yet through the web is heard
"You are loved."
"You are loved,
says the flame of the Spirit.
"YOU are loved,
"You ARE loved,
"You are LOVED,"
repeats the flame of the Spirit,
until the soul is warmed,
and can say for itself,
"I am loved."

No longer afraid of being used by others,
the soul is free,
free to be tenderly affirming,
encouraging,
enjoying,
loving,
free to say to another,
"You are loved."

Then tears are allowed to flow,
softening,
releasing deep feelings,
turning grievance to grief,
watering seeds that blossom into joy.
New life begins...

We recall that Peter wept.
He had followed Jesus after his arrest,
compelled by love,
by closeness.
"I'll never leave you."
Peter's strong body was used to risk,
toughened by storms that rent mast, sail, net.
"I'll never leave you."
But as he waited by the fire,
a girl's voice said,
"You're one of them!"
"No!" defended Peter –
and fled.
She had touched the fearful man
inside the strong exterior.
Peter wept.
That pure beautiful love was betrayed:
Peter wept.

For us too
the tough exterior hides the fear within
Tears reluctant to come
roar from the depths of our guts,
tearing,
bruising,
shaking the body
that has concreted the sadness securely inside,
cracking the block,
shattering,
revealing it was not made from solid tears.

These tears were not allowed to flow
by the child
bravely responding
to the voice that said,
"Be brave – don't upset your father."
The child must accept its cage.
Keep quiet – or be rejected.
Find comfort in food.
Find comfort in imaginary worlds.

Yet there is no escape from the spirit that says,
"You are loved,
you are loved,
you are loved."

The voice insists again and again
until the child within
dares to be held,
dares to say,
"I am loved."

"I am afraid."
"I am not always brave."
"I am not always strong."

Then tears are allowed to flow.
The rigid blocks of past training
shatter.
Old resentments are freed
and cleansed.
Vulnerable humanity celebrates.
New life begins...

Receive the gift of tears.

## 2 *I wanted...*

THE new life revealed the pressures and conditioning of earlier life: the values of perfection, control, and idealism of our western patriarchal society that I had wholeheartedly tried to serve, at the price of damaging myself.

The healing began with anger at the injustice. I apologize to those who received the projections of my wrath, and I am grateful to them for helping me to 'warm up' and get my energies going.

Healing continued as I found my self-esteem. Finally, the deep cleansing of the wounds came through a holy man, who in the strength of the Vulnerable Christ faced my damaged feminine with his masculine image. While I know he had the security of the counselling room, he still had to give authentically of himself.

The following 'Confession of a daughter of patriarchy, and her absolving' was written in gratitude to him for his courage and compassion.

I wanted to be idealized...

... just like the Virgin,
still,
serene,
the perfect container,
not flinching when he had his way.
(Perfect Mother with Perfect Babe:
Perfect Father is mothered too.)

... just like the whore redeemed:
sexual delight,
with power to give life,
strengthened by the beloved.

But I became a little woman in a big shell,
nervous,
self-critical,
guilty,
self-destructive.
Black clouds enveloped me:
I became the mad woman,
the witch,
the whore,
the s-mother,
the spider.

One man risked hearing, seeing.
Bravely he faced the evils,
touched them,
risked the pain they could inflict on him,
went through the ugly shell,
held the small person.

I began to live:
I heard my name for the first time.

He shone beams of sunshine on me,
weeded,
pruned,
turned weeds to flowers.

By his courage,
by his deep compassion,
I am being absolved.

I wanted approval.

Good daughters please,
serve fathers well,
mustn't upset people,
give to others,
don't expect to receive,
express woman's role through food:
nurture is a woman's job –
men can't nurture.

Only we have the power.
We are told we must use it.
But I am drained of being –
give, give, give.
"Give more, give more."
"Feed us, feed us."
Giant 'hims' –
feeble 'hers' –
such are the archetypes.

The holy man hears,
says, "Stop it."
He admits an 'unconscious man' in himself.
A light flickers inside.
"I love you," I respond.

But the journey to wholeness is long,
the flame that cleanses hurts.
Grievance,
old habits,
reticence,
they leave much to be burnt out.

And the holy man hurts,
struggles too.
By pain we are being absolved.

"Your body is for him."

They said it disturbs him.
He will use it as he needs.
His need mustn't be denied.

Where is my body?
Little awareness is left.
It grows heavy for self-protection.

The vulnerable man makes no demands –
only a gentle touch,
a steady strength.
I may hide in his body,
admit my grief.
He warms me.
I live,
I dance,
I draw.
By his body I am being absolved.

"Man is dominant,
woman submits."
That was my conditioning
whilst receiving the education of a son.

My inner voice said,
"Play their game."
"Be passive."
"Cope with your head."
"Learn to escape."
"Don't heed the crippling."
As my body and mind split,
feelings diffused into chaos,
rejection,
fear, anxiety, deadness.

And another power emerged –
erotic –
to weave,
to invite,
to control,
to manage,
to manipulate.

"She who shall be obeyed" emerged –
destruction,
passivity,
eroticism,
deadness,
destruction.

The holy man risks meeting the Gorgon.
"Will you feel cherished?"
"I hurt when you don't trust me."
I learn to trust,
I learn to give,
I learn to receive.
Split parts of me are drawing together,
freeing me to know my own woundings.
I am being absolved by wholiness.

# 3 *Outcast child returns*

SCAR tissue continues to prickle, and many buds form before flowers open. The child within me had been buried along with the other feelings. Her distorted image was either of a heavy fiery beast or of a rag doll. But as the truer image took shape, I knew my outcast child was tenderness.

My outcast child was tenderness.

I need her now.
I call her from hiding,
burial,
banishment.
She was rejected.
I rejected her.
Where is God?

God is with the outcast child.
I hear him say to her,
"Mary, you are sensitive."

I greet her,
back, back from the days before her memory,
washed in the waterfalls of birth,
laughing,
gentle,
alive.

# 4 *My dagger*

THE long suppressed image of my own feminine was distorted too. The self-giving of 'good daughters', 'good wives', 'good mothers', when taken to extreme, gives power to others. The woman is left passive, cut off, as in a box that contains her in the role she is to fulfil.

As I watch and grow closer to men, I feel many of them carry this damage too – in their animas, their inner female imagery that has been contained, repressed, and punished. The feminine image in man is very damaged.

However, woman still has human energy of her own which may be left to eat away inside her, making her nervous, lacking in confidence. Or it may find ways of sneaking out. Perhaps she will become a manipulative 'she – who – will – be – obeyed'. Perhaps she will, like me, hide away a dagger in the box. And on the occasional skirmish it flashes into action.

I have long carried a dagger.
It cuts well.
It is patterned from my early days
with signs and symbols
that give authority to others –
not to me.
'They' will always know more than I.
'They' are to be served, upheld.

My dagger flashes into action
by my own energy
that knows I exist
and have a contribution to make.

The dagger cuts through the box I am held in:
it waits,
'setting up' the scene
into which it will flash,
'show up',
cut open,
expose,
hurt others.

I will own my dagger,
hold it in my hands,
let it be seen,
with the crippling of the box,
the grief of lost life,
and with the truth and love
that leads me to Peace.

# 5 *Hold me*

I RECALL that my most arid times in the desert have been relieved by physical sensation whilst praying. I am amazed and humbled by these gifts that have come through my body. So I write *Hold me* – body experiences in prayer.

A five-year old was afraid of the bombs.
They said,
"You can talk to Jesus."
I asked,
"Hold me."

I felt a Hand on my shoulder.
I did not want to move all night.
I wasn't surprised.
I said,
"Thank you."
And I knew I was all right.

A lonely young woman,
vibrant,
rejected,
fearful,
self-loathing,
I prayed,
"Hold me."

I found I was enfolded with strength and warmth,
and I said to myself,
"I do matter –
I will go on."

An exhausted mother of three
prays by the bed of a sleeping child,
"I have nothing left to give them:
hold me."

His warmth,
gentle,
permanent,
is in front of me,
to draw me to life,
to receive confidence,
to be myself.

Middle-aged,
with increasing pain as I bore the curse,
proud of denying it,
rising above it,
practical,
'sensible',
alone,
I buried my face in a mossy bank
and sobbed,
"I have had enough:
hold me."

And Father's daughter that I was,
I yielded to Mother Earth.
She received my body,
and I knew the truth of my body too,
blessed,
desirable,
just as it was.
No more pain!

A clergy woman in a man's Church,
I tired of struggling lovingly with my enemies.
"Hold me,"
I prayed.
And She did –
two woman's hands in my middle back.

I relax,
rest on her.
She is strong,
full of love and grief.
Her power goes with me.

Did She hold Mary of Nazareth,
unnoticed,
unnamed?

# 6 *In Christ there are no witches*

As I became more at home in my female body, I discovered I had two womanly self-images. One was a pale, greying, ageing woman, as dried up as the desert. The other was a witch. This frightened and excited me. I discovered the witch could use her energy to 'be-witch', that is to exercise power over other people. Yet, when I owned that power and used it responsibly, it was very creative, no longer dangerous. Through openness to Christ the redeemed witch and the grey woman have come together, healed, strong, and at one. So I wrote, *In Christ there are no witches*. This leads me to ask men, "Is the witch you fear actually in you, in your imagery, or in me? Can you dare to open your feelings in prayer?"

I glimpsed her
behind the familiar folk,
neglected,
pale,
grieving,
head high,
looking sideways.
I knew her.
For I hear her deep intuitive insights,
I experience her evoking powers at crossroads,
I know her fear of persecution and denial.
"Your powers are dangerous," they say.
"You may not exist."

She does exist –
where shall she go?

Fly round the edges
where she is safer and alive?
'Weaving chaos' they call that.

Watching opportunities to fly in and use her powers?
'Sneaky and manipulative,' they call that.

Focus her powers, draw others to her?
'Bewitching,' they call that.

I held out my hands,
"Woman, you are in me.
I want to love you.
Come..."

She could hardly move,
so long had she been there.
I grieved and sobbed for us.
Assured,
fed,
warmed,
she grew stronger,
younger
beautiful.

And then I hung back!
Why change?
The Destroyed became for me the Destroyer.
Life is comfortable without her.
Forbidding voices echo from the past:
"Be good."
"Be like us."
"Father knows best."
Should I bury her again?

Christ's fool reaches out,
warms my heart with steady hand.

I trust.
I can greet her,
I can share her with others.
We don't have to hide.
And she comes close,
fair,
alive,
effective.
I receive her gifts openly,
delightful,
unfamiliar.
Now there is no more skirmishing in the dark.
I grow stronger.
She gives free choice,
accuracy of loving,
creates new life.

I need her life energy to share with others.
For we are all weak,
serving and caring only like well controlled mothers.

Listen, men and women,
my female ego is free to be!
I embrace her, my Guardian Angel.
In Christ there are no witches.

# 7 *Whom does the grail serve?*

WHILE the female is hurt, she holds back, protects herself, does not freely mingle with the masculine in herself or in men.

I discovered, as I became more sure of my feminine, that I could let go of the grief and grievance which I had used to protect my wounded self. Then I related more easily with the masculine, in men and women and myself.

The process in me was reminiscent of the old story of the Holy Grail from the tales of King Arthur. So I adapted the story to speak of the wounded feminine at this end of the twentieth century.

In the Strong-Hold castle,
in the centre of the Kingdom,
old Fisher-Queen sat heavily,
guarding the Loving-Cup,
filled with wine long fermented
of the masculine and the feminine life of Christ.

The land was barren, dried up, hardened, violent.
Neither in life sexual nor in life spiritual
did much blossom or bear fruit.

The Jester searched the land for the Loving-Cup.
At first he was confident, self-assured.
Then he lost his tools,
and could give only of himself.
He found the castle, entered, saw the Queen.
His eyes penetrated the life-source within her.
Life rose through her in a song,
pierced the heavy wound of grief
that surrounded her heart,
the wound of denial,
of refusal of her female body and being.
The scar tissue released its grip.
Water and blood flowed free.
The old Queen is free to die.
The Loving-Cup is free.

The Jester asks,
"Whom does the Grail serve?"
The Loving-Cup moves out of the castle,
available for all who will drink, men and women.
The wine of feminine and masculine ferment is free
to bring life to the land.
Earth, water, air, fire,
all mingle in harmony.
There is flowering and fruiting!

# 8 *Waiting...*

I AM becoming a worshipping, sexual, human being. I am an alien in the Tradition of the Church that holds my faith in Christ. Out of doors, I worship incompletely. So I can only wait, only be faithful to everyday reality, to the desert, and to our incompleteness in our Infinite God. The following came out of a workshop on sexuality and spirituality.

Out of doors I grow steady as a tree –
    rooted in the earth,
    reaching to the sky –
        FREE
But I'm not a tree.

In the Abbey I hurt from rigid stones –
    feminine denied by straight lines,
    men's voices echo round –
        COLD
And I cannot be me.

On the steps, by the loos –
    I wait under-ground,
    surrounded by humble basic things –
        I AM ME
And in God, I am who I shall be.

# FLOWERS –
# NOW AND THEN

# 9 *Beginning to move*

As we dare to let our true feelings flow, there are 'flowers' to be found. I shall always be grateful that I started on my inner journey. And I shall never forget the pain of it.

I knew only heaviness –
from hidden anxiety,
grief,
hate,
fear.

I glimpse light in an alert, sensitive face,
I sense hope in a tension-racked body,
I long to touch him,
follow his path –

kept from me that I might find my own.

Reluctantly I move into dark spaces,
let go a little,
encouraged by his trust
to face shadows
and hear dreams.

# 10 *Journeying*

In time I learned to trust my feelings and let them be creative.

My map shapes behind me
to identify where I've been.

Now and again I stop,
gather powers and feelings in my inner space,
hold them focused in my being,
to move,
re-shape,
come to birth,
just as they shall be,
strong or puny.

And I journey on.

## 11 *Creating margins*

I LEARNED the freedom and creativity of being on the margins of the Church and Society. And I learn to make my contribution willingly from there.

"You may not..."
"You ought to..."
"You can only..."

Says the Centre,
rigidly committed to success –
and dying.

"But I am..."
"I can..."
"I do..."

Says the Margin,
alive,
free from the Centre,
whose expectations it cannot meet.

"I can give you life,"

Says the Margin,
willing to give to the Centre who parented it –

Yet fearfully –

For,
"I shall take a little from you,"

Says part of the Centre.

"Ouch, a bit of me has gone,"

Says the Margin.

"Mmm, I feel better for that,"

Says the Centre.

## 12 *Feminine redeemed*

As I work with women, guiding their inner journeys a little, I notice their long, hidden, primal feminine energy being recognized within them. Here are two examples: images of the feminine received – the butterfly and the swan.

Long she rested within her own inner larva skin,
dried,
unshaped,
sleeping.

Slowly she opened:
her inner butterfly,
new and moist,
came to her.

They rested together in the Sun;
she let the butterfly reach her inner being.

And there SHE was,
Creator, Redeemer, Sustainer Being –
Beautiful, Perfect Love.

And as she walked under the trees
she knew Christ is Risen.


She was folded round her guilt,
buried alive,
screaming.

As she warmed a little,
in her inner being,
her Swan came through the wall to her,
to lead her,
to swim with her,

Until she became beautiful again,
acceptable,
forgiven,
her feminine dignity restored.

Now she and the Swan are one.

## 13 *Men's feelings redeemed*

MEN are learning to recognize and live through their feelings, to make space in relationships for others to find their feelings. There is a flowering here and there among man-kind.

They said he was like a dolphin.
Others said,
"Dolphins treat depression."

He moves in a flash,
speeding to a situation.

The smile of his eyes
penetrates deep.

Suspended,
he holds short of the goal,
waits,
invites life from the other.

He stands on his tail:
flapping fins encourage.

"Come come,"
his being says.
Urgent gentleness
draws movement from the depths.

# 14 *True feelings emerge*

WE have been conditioned to fit roles and stereotypes of society, trained to play our part, often at the cost of not knowing our true feelings. But though they are largely hidden they do not always stay concealed. They emerge unexpectedly, unidentified, to frighten and confuse us.

As she talks of her friends,
I 'see' dolls, puppets,
arranged, watched, played with.

She turns herself into an object,
and joins them.

She dare not live any other way.
She seeks the safety of control,
each role certain, played out.

I ache for the real life,
cut off, locked away, dried up,
in these victims of our 'civilization'.


He is gentle, sensitive, vulnerable,
cautious of women:
they can devour him,
molest, humiliate him.

Later – he finds –

He can make household decisions,
have some authority in her domain!
He can defend himself when she argues,
feel violent towards her,
for self-preservation!


The child called out in her,
"I'm screaming, I'm frightened."
But she is an adult woman, too, whom I love,
And in trepidation
I faced her demanding and said,
"I know she is in you,
you must care for her."
She was angry.
We waited...
Slowly she is owning her child.

## 15 *True feelings heal*

TOGETHER with friends I have found healing by owning contradictory feelings. We explored one way of doing this by reflecting on animals, as in the imagery of the holy mountain in Isaiah chapter 11.

Tigress,
hunting with fiery eyes penetrating the darkness,
terrorizing those who hurt you:
Gazelle,
fragile, camouflaged,
fearing violation by beast and man:
*Come, O Child, call them both:*
*the Tigress and the Gazelle.*
*They need each other's strength,*
*on the slopes of the holy mountain.*

Lioness,
lithe body pounding through your space,
roar, and with accurate paws,
kill, protect, play:
Ewe-Lamb,
spindly legs quivering,
helpless, woolly body bleating,
suckled, nuzzled, coming to life
to graze, frisk, play:
*Come, O Child, call them both:*
*the Lioness and the Lamb*
*lie down together*
*on the slopes of the holy mountain.*

# 16 *True caring*

FOR generations women have found ways to be strong, to manage men and situations. We have not always been truthful and loving in our relationships. We have perpetuated deception, the battle of the sexes, and a destructive 'loving' that uses power over others rather than holds power for them.

She assumes I need her support,
her pity.
'Sisterly' she calls it.

To her I'm vulnerable.
I do not work in the centre of things,
I do not handle, humour, men.
I do not boss 'little boys'
and 'make them happy'.
I am not managing men,
sweetly, manipulatively, serving them.
I must be helpless –
by her sights!

I reply to her,
"Oh no, it is you who are vulnerable.
Your energies are indirectly aggressive,
manipulative.
You would be stronger if you were real.
Do you know what you feel?
Try the power of making your contribution –
assertive we call it!"

# 17 *Fears*

THE expectations about life that we hold for ourselves and for others become exaggerated. They grip us and distance us from the truth. Healing begins to come only when we are honest about our real feelings.

The haunting howl of the wolf
in the dark forest,
menacing...
Fear runs through our veins.
Will he attack us,
savage us?

"No!" says the wise one,
"She is crying for her dead babe."

But the fear still surges through
from our innermost beings.

Our babes cannot die.
We will not admit such mortality!
"Mother must be successful,
mustn't let us die!"

Such anguish is not part of our success story:
we plan comfort and security.
We cannot be helpless,
without control,
Such primal cries call the primitive creature in us,
whose cry we do not wish to hear.
She echoes our laments,
our loss of mother, father, friend, lover.

This evil is rooted in our own fear,
born of anxieties about ambitions
to control, succeed.

And do we fear creating nothing?
Of leaving no impress on the earth?
Of being nothing?

# 18 *Knowing our needs*

WE can always create something new in ourselves when we are truthful and stick with the chaos, pain, and love which truth brings. Needs felt and openly named find the caring they need, through controlled touch, imagination, eye contact, words, which do not demand a complete relationship with another person. It is enough to receive and heal within ourselves, without demanding total commitment from another – and without desperately grabbing at relationships to satisfy our partially identified lack or need. We need not resort to fantasy either, if we learn to become steady, to receive from others, and to trust ourselves to make space for others and for ourselves. This is the Way of true loving. We do not need to pretend to be perfect and get it right for others all the time.

Intimacy –
eyes –
touch –
together –
mingled.

Moments –
open –
something new
is made
from within us.

Space –
new shapes
form
in each of us.

Dare I open myself?
Am I stable enough
not to grab,
or drown?

Can you let go too?
Do we trust each other?

I wish –
I will –
power to be,
and to let be.

We can hold opposites –
and create something new.

Anger held with a little love
shapes into compassion.

Grief held with a loving hope,
turns to joy.

Fear admitted,
faced with love around,
turns to trust.

We invoked the feelings
in our bodies,
held the opposites within,
moved and prayed,
and received new feelings.

Our heads noted,
valued,
marked,
our discovery of feelings.

There is always time,
at any stage of life,
to receive what we need,
letting healing come
from naming the need,
drawing into wholeness
that which was missing years ago.

The girl could not be close to her father,
that he might be open to her,
letting his masculine celebrate her feminine,
draw her to womanhood.
Now the woman lets her inner girl
receive gentle, fatherly masculine.

The boy could not be close to his father,
that he might be open to him,
letting his masculine mirror strength to his son,
draw him to manhood.
Now the man lets his inner boy
receive steady firmness of fatherly masculine.

The girl could not be close to her mother,
that she might receive her,
letting her feminine model and mould her daughter,
draw her to womanhood.
Now the woman lets her inner girl
receive true feminine energy.

The boy could not be close to his mother,
that she might receive him,
letting her feminine gentle, enliven, free her son,
draw him to manhood.
Now the man lets his inner boy
receive security, warmth, inspiration of woman.

# 19 *Towards wholeness of humanity*

WESTERN Civilization has developed in such a way that masculine, dominant, thrusting energy is highly valued, and feminine energy is controlled, subdued, and valued for its passivity. Consequently, feminine energy becomes either weak or monstrous. This distortion is destructive of human beings and communities. As we recognize the denial of human-beingness that happens when we serve stereotyped roles, we free ourselves from their power and move towards respect, love, and peace in and between people.

I asked,
"Was the feminine that men fear, deny, control in me,
was it really in You?
"Was the Divine Feminine in You?"
Christ laughed, and LAUGHED, and LAUGHED.
"All is redeemed.
In the Garden of innocence,
where nakedness is not named,
there is still flowering and fruiting,
Be in my love –
know die-ing, fermenting, rising."

Later,
I watched close rank
of ecclesiastical brotherhood.
"Heresy!" I shouted.
"You have ruined Paradise
by splitting us one from another,
making layer upon layer
of artificial roles, stereotypes, games,
and calling them 'God's will'.
Return to innocence.
Use your strength to hold, value, steady.
Use your minds to affirm and gently shape.
Use your bodies to give life.
Receive life from me.
I can draw life into you,
I can hold and shape something for you.
Let us dance together in Christ,
and there will be flowering and fruiting again.
Know that Christ laughed!"

Mighty Bull,
fathering the herd,
thundering past with weight and noise,
trampling the tiny things around you:
Skylark,
desperate,
hovering and crying to decoy him,
protecting her nest on the ground
from his lumbering hooves:
*Come, O Child, call them both:*
*the Bull will steady,*
*the Lark shall sing,*
*on the slopes of the holy mountain.*

He-Calf,
imprisoned in darkened shed,
your flesh kept white
to pleasure those who feast on you:
Great She-Bear,
giving birth in darkened cave,
waiting through winter,
venturing forth in spring,
killing for her cubs
who feed, play, grow:
*Come, O Child, call them both:*
*the Bear grows gentler,*
*the Calf finds strength,*
*on the slopes of the holy mountain.*

They meet –

The fat man stands still,
looks strong,
but his little dog hangs back.

The small lady keeps walking,
politely helpless.
But her large black dog charges past.

The fat man relaxes.
His dog has expressed their feelings.

The small lady smiles.
She and her dog are of one mind.

Their baby son had died.
The love that made him held them together –
yet in such different places.
She knows love from birthing,
giving new life.
She knows the risk,
the vale of death
all mothers and babes pass through
in their separating.
She knows the earth
which sustains them
and where her babe's body now belongs.
Her grief is beautifully laced with love.

He knows helplessness,
from having nothing to do,
not able to give,
to improve.
His body cries out,
"It's not fair."
His grief is dark,
held nobly within.

She reaches out from her strength.
He comes to her with his pain.
For a moment he is their son,
she is mother.
And her body is weak –
she needs his strength.

Love's patterns weave.
The Creator Love works in them still.

# 20 *Primary feminine*

WOMEN who are unshaped by education in the white male system in which we live hold for all of us feminine energy that gives life. Other women gain strength from this real, body-based feminine. They learn that their true power is not in their 'animus'. (Men find their creativity by coming to know their 'anima'.) as feminine strength develops in men and women, the battle of the sexes decreases. For their strengths are clearly, cleanly matched. No more is it a matter of conquer or be conquered, manage or manipulate. Rather is there complementariness, creativity, harmony.

Here is cosmic healing, healing for communities, families, individuals. But it takes courage, time, patience, and energy to claim one's own power of body, mind, soul, and spirit in Christ, to struggle with our enemies, and to live through the chaos of the dying of old patterns and the transformation to the new.

Her feminine is strong.
Her intelligence is natural,
unshaped in masculine form
by academic institutions.
She thinks with her body,
sensing appropriateness.

Their feminine is largely hidden,
educated as they are,
trained for careers in the man's world.
Their bodies are starved into submission,
or padded for protection and comfort.

She holds for them the hidden images,
Earth Mother, Virgin, Sacred Whore.
As they search for their real feelings,
they are finding their feminine egos.

They are finding freedom,
strength of truth.
The hidden energies of the feminine
are released.
The feminine begins to dance with the masculine:
cosmic balance and harmony are being restored.

Men and women agreed:
We both mother, create,
in our wombs,
in the cells of our bodies.
We birth with joy – and death.


Let your surface rhythms be held
by the deep, steady rhythms of the universe.

Trust who you are,
where you are, in confidence,
watching the rhythms of those around you.

# BLOSSOMS GIVEN

## 21 *Look again*

CLAIMING power from real feminine energy, as experienced in women's bodies and experience, their feelings, and relationships, frees souls and minds of both men and women to discern the gifts of our Infinite God. 'Blossoms' I call these gifts, for they hold the beauty of Truth, and their fulness is a part of Glory. We come to places in the desert journey – could they be oases? – where variety flourishes and differences in and between people are enhancing. These places of richness require us to take a stronger, clearer look at our view of Truth, for in the past we may well have seen mirages, not oases.

Someone asked,

Since male and female are made in God's image,
and male and female are redeemed in Christ,

Is there really neither male nor female in Christ?

No, there is both male and female in Christ.

## 22 *Christ looked at me...*

WE meet Jesus Christ in new ways as we grow and heal. Not least, the feminine in Jesus holds, gives life, transforms, and sends forth those who ask for healing.

My heart was warmly resting on my anger.
I picked up a stone to hurl.
Christ looked at me – with aching loving face.
I put down the stone and the anger.
And I knew Christ's life moving and working in me,
in my female body.

It was the worldly voices that said,
"You are the same as a man."


I knew my blindness.

I was not sure I was made in the image of God.

"Jesus," I called.
But the inner voices shouted louder,
"God is male."
"Mary is a woman – she is not God."
"Jesus is a male saviour."
"God is Father."
"Deny your feminine body."


In the chaos I called louder.
Jesus turned.
Our eyes met.
"You are loved,
body, mind, soul, and spirit."
So said his eyes.

As warmth spreads through me,
I say,
"I can see:
I *am* made in the image of God."

## 23  *Gifts while we sleep*

THE sadnesses, the fears, and the anxieties which we repress come to consciousness through dreams. By learning to interpret the images in dreams, we receive gifts of feeling, energy, and understanding that help our healing and growth.

A deep dream brought encouragement for my spiritual journey in female body.

From the depths of unknowing
came a girl-child,
lying in a manger.

Christ,
imaging His Mother,
is the babe's mother.

Ordinary folk greet her –
mothers, fathers, relations.

'Wise men' are unrecognizable.
But gold, frankincense, and myrrh
tell of the spiritual journey she must make.

## 24 *Martha and Mary*

NEW awareness of body, heart, and mind brings new experience into prayer. Old understandings change. I found that imaginative contemplation based on Scripture can bring new insights, new gifts of the Spirit. Martha and Mary changed for me.

*From contemplation on Luke* 10.38-42

Mary sat at Jesus' feet,
her body filled with anticipation,
her face alight.
Her energy flowed.

No wonder Martha complained
about Mary not working.

*From contemplation on John* 11.17*ff*

Martha said,
"My brother is dead."

"Jesus,
I've come to meet you to ask,
Come to him.
There is no life.
He's bound up
in darkness,
stone cold,
inside rock."

"You could have saved him."

"God will give what you ask."

Jesus said,

"I came."

"Your brother will rise again.
Do you believe?"

Martha declared,
"You are the Christ,
who is coming into the world."

We too may pray for our brothers,
buried under patriarchy.

## 25 *New life*

WE are called to follow Christ, to begin to live as Jesus lived. Again I have found imaginative contemplation on Scripture helpful. I shared something of my experience of life with Christ. I found a few surprises, not least that I need not be fixed in woman's traditional role.

*From contemplation on Mark* 14.3 *ff*

He massaged my head with loving care.
Energy flowed.

Taking such trust and peace into my body,
I could even face my own death.

I have great news for the poor in spirit.
Receive anointing – as Christ does.

*From contemplation on Luke 7.36ff*

As I talked with the efficient, detached man,
my feelings ceased to flow.
There was little exchanged between us.

A hurt, confused woman slipped in,
soothed my feet with her tears,
releasing her feelings – and mine.

And energy flowed through my body.
I lifted her face,
and let her love flow back from me to her.

"Women!" the detached man exclaimed.
(He is uneasy cut off from life's flow.)
We said, "Learn to live like us."

# 26 *Fall redeemed*

DUALISM has bedevilled our theology. We are only just learning that a rich and exuberant creation can hold variety. When we choose, we do not always have to make choices between good or bad, up or down, you or me. Where there are differences, we can say 'and' rather than 'or'. Christ redeems all, even the Fall! In our faith we must be willing to receive that redemption. The New Adam and the New Eve in men and women move away from dualism. Their lives are complementary – 'and... and' – and they discover that much is blossoming.

Eve saw that the fruit of the tree of knowledge was good.
She gave Adam the apple,
the knowledge of good and evil.
From then on choices had to be made –
for success, achievement, perfection,
or for chaos and destruction.
The responsibility of choice
brings fear, anxiety, guilt.
Eve focused her anxiety on her body –
the pain and stress of the curse and of childbirth.
Adam worked harder and harder to achieve.
The tree of life was guarded and kept from both of them.

Darkness prevailed.

Out of the darkness came the Light.
The New Adam and the New Eve
now shared the tree of life,
mingling roots and sinews and fluids.
And they knew the space between them,
neither possessing nor being possessed.
Here was no pressure for perfection,
only the need for what is appropriate.
She relaxed into her body;
pain and stress faded away.
He delighted in being creative;
he felt light-hearted again.
The Fall is redeemed.
They bless the Creator!

# 27 *Temptations re-appear*

INCREASING awareness of feminine energy brings new temptation, and reveals old temptations more clearly. We need the Christ who holds the distortions of our humanity together with the Light of Love.

In the wilderness

I am tempted
to feed on my grievance,
to protest,
to seek power.

But I will listen to the Word of God:
"Love me,
love your neighbour,
love your enemy."

I am tempted
to say from the heights of religion,
"See how free *I* am" –
playing on the virtue of my salvation.

But I will not tempt God.
I will journey with others,
that we might find wholeness.

I am tempted
to 'mother',
to 'bewitch',
to use others' needs,
to claim power over them.

But I would worship God – only –
the One who holds together
human distortion and love,

that we might grow.

## 28 *Take up your cross*

SHOUTING about injustice is not enough. We cannot heal by insisting that others change. They are more likely to change as they experience the truth of our healing.

Jesus Christ,
as I accompany you
through your Passion,
and name the denial
of my feminine body,
of my feminine identity,
I own my complicity in the betrayal.

I accept the pain of my wounds...

And waiting,
I embody my anger
to give me power
to die to the past.
No more leading a double life.
For I recognize myself.
The early years have given up their fears.
New life begins.

Alleluia! Alleluia!

So be it. Amen.

## 29 *In bread and wine*

JESUS gave us symbols of his body and blood – bread and wine. The processes involved in the making of bread and wine hold the truth of his life. The bread begins with seed, which is nurtured in the earth that it may grow into a mature plant which produces grain. The grain is mixed with other grains, ground down to flour, mixed with water and yeast to be heated, transformed in shape, and turned into bread to feed people. All human beings can live this full process of growth, of maturing, of giving for change into a new formation, of giving for others, especially when fed by the Spirit of Christ.

Likewise wine holds the crushing of the fruit, the waiting, the fermenting that new life may bubble through. We take in this symbol of Christ, that we may be open to the process of living the crushing changes, the waiting, and the yielding to the fermenting that new life energy will rise. Joy does come.

Both processes are familiar to us. In earlier religions grain and bread, grapes and wine, were symbols of the goddess. Was Jesus aware that they included this expression of feminine experience? We cannot know the answer to that question, but, when redeemed through Christ, these symbols deeply inform us of our Infinite God and are available to deepen our worship.

May the wine of the Divine Feminine
be created in you,
as it was in Christ,
as it was in Mary of Magdala.
Her beloved died.
Her desire for him,
and her newly healed self,
descended to ferment.

May the wine of the Divine Feminine
flow through you,
as it flowed through Christ,
as it flowed through Mary of Magdala.
She knew him still,
in her own separateness,
and from her depths
new wine rose.

May the wine of the Divine Feminine
send you forth,
as it helped send Mary of Magdala.
They touched for a moment –
companion lovers –
and she is free to tell,
"Love is risen."

# 30 *Holy images uncovered*

TRUTH held in feminine images has been hidden, denied, distorted, along with the feminine itself. As one example, we had almost lost the image of 'owl-eyes' as a symbol of the Divine Feminine. Reclaiming these images in Christ helps heal the splits, distortions, and imbalances of sexual imagery. But in no way do these images stand on their own as God. To claim so would be as idolatrous as exalting any image, all of which can become narrow and limiting. They do, however, make available to us a greater variety of images of God for our understanding and our prayer.

May the owl-eyes of the Divine Feminine
look on you,
as they looked on vulnerable, strong Mary,
birthing in a stable;
as they looked on gentle, strong Joseph,
standing by; as they looked on the Son,
born for sacrifice,
that earth may receive new life.

And may her Power flow through you, (N),
this Christmas-tide
and every day.

Earth Mother, home of all,
held in the arms and hands of Creator God,
eternally bringing new birth
through your spiralling,
earth our being.

Virgin, earthed by Mother,
yet beautiful, free, yearning
for impregnation of Truth
that will create new life,
make New Life in us.

Sacred Whore, steadied by the Virgin,
held in wholesome goodness by Mother,
honestly respond to your hunger
with love, play, humour, tears,
that through your passion,
we may evoke life.

Giver of life,
Infinite God,
penetrating and containing,
gestating and birthing,
open our being to Yours.

Bearer of pain,
Gracious Beloved,
seeded with Truth,
yearning, dying for new life,
open our being to Yours.

Maker of love,
hungry and passionate,
refining and enlivening,
guiding and inspiring,
open our being to Yours.

Holy Trinity,
looking at one another,
earthing and impregnating,
evoking life between You,
open our being to Yours.

# 31
## Opened and widened, so we worship

To Thou who art who Thou shalt be,
I open wide my soul:
Thou art in me, and I in Thee,
Thus known, I am made whole.

To each Christ gives the face of Truth:
I own my twists from grace.
Thou art in me and I in Thee,
Thus known, I feel Thy space.

[*Can be sung to the tune 'Epsom'*]

COME Thou the Space within my soul,
Where I conceive and hold
The Love that shapes, unseen transforms,
The Love that will re-mould.

Be Thou the Space between Thy folk,
Our Chalice, sanctified.
Love dies and grieves, yet lives for all,
The Love that's not denied.

Be Thou the Space from which I move,
Am birthed anew from strife,
Filled by Thine own transforming bliss,
The Love that seeds my life.

[*Can be sung to the tune 'Abridge'*]

WE trust in Thee, Thou ent'rest deep within us,
We enter deep in Thee, yet space we know.
Thou-He, Thou-She, for Thou art Thou who shalt be,
We live in Thee and in Thine heart we grow.

[*Can be sung to the tune 'Finlandia'*]

We celebrate life.
Look at our many original blessings –
earth, trees, flowers,
air, water,

fire that burns in us, around us,
warming friendships,
consuming, refining, consummating.

We delight in the making of our souls,
by letting go our inner defences,
by allowing healing to our hurts,
by trusting our bodies,
as we follow Jesus the Christ,
Pioneer of the Holy Way of Life,
to dance in the Love that is God.

"I will never forget you,"
says the Infinite Lover,
Thou-She, Thou-He.
"I will penetrate your being.
"I will hold you alive,
and growing in my womb space.
"I will firmly steady and contain you all.
"I will send you forth transformed."

Received, may we receive –
Nutured, may we nurture –
Enclosed, may we enclose –
Sent forth, may we send forth –
In the power of the Creator,
the Christ, and the Holy Spirit.
Amen.